# the ART
## OF
## LAP DANCING

# the Art
# of
# Lap Dancing

STERLING

New York / London
www.sterlingpublishing.com

STERLING and the distinctive Sterling logo are registered trademarks of
Sterling Publishing Co., Inc.

**Library of Congress Cataloging-in-Publication Data Available**

10  9  8  7  6  5  4  3  2  1

Published by Sterling Publishing Co., Inc.
387 Park Avenue South, New York, NY 10016
© 2008 by Peekaboo Pole Dancing Ltd.
Distributed in Canada by Sterling Publishing
C/o Canadian Manda Group, 165 Dufferin Street
Toronto, Ontario, Canada M6K 3H6
Distributed in the United Kingdom by GMC Distribution Services
Castle Place, 166 High Street, Lewes, East Sussex, England BN7 1XU
Distributed in Australia by Capricorn Link (Australia) Pty. Ltd.
P.O. Box 704, Windsor, NSW 2756, Australia

Printed in China

Sterling ISBN-13: 978-1-4027-5487-6
          ISBN-10: 1-4027-5487-6

For information about custom editions, special sales, premium and
corporate purchases, please contact Sterling Special Sales
Department at 800-805-5489 or specialsales@sterlingpublishing.com.

# Contents

It's been a blast, but we've gotta go. And
remember, hon, practice makes purrrrfect!

# the ART
## OF
## LAP DANCING

# Dance to the Music

You want to get in shape and look fabulous, right? But wouldn't it be cool to have some sexy fun at the same time? With *The Art of Lap Dancing*, you can do just that.

Hello, everyone; Peekaboo here. We'd like to take this opportunity to introduce the red-hot sequel to our best-selling book on pole dancing.

It's called *The Art of Lap Dancing*, and it's our super-foxy guide to the dance craze that's sweeping the nation.

Read on now for more about lap dancing and what it can do for your love life. Check out the fitness benefits. Then move on to the preparation tips and professionally choreographed moves.

There's even expert fashion advice on hand from our five mischievous Peekaboo Girls.

All in all, it's everything you need to sculpt your body and tease your man at the same time.

# The Art of Lap Dancing Uncovered

Showing off your sexy side. Making your man completely gaga. Getting your hottest-ever body...There's certainly no shortage of reasons to make lap dancing your new favorite pastime....

Here at Peekaboo, we think there's an irresistible lap dancer in everyone. In fact, we're sure of it. And our aim is to unleash yours upon an unsuspecting world.

The techniques that follow are tailor-made for you to express your sexuality in a positive way.

When you perform a lap dance for your man, you'll be the one with the power. You'll feel so naughty. So sexy. So incredibly irresistible. And he'll be left begging for more.

What's more, wiggling and jiggling have never been so much fun. A good lap-dancing session is the equivalent of a fun workout. You'll be exercising muscles you never even knew you had!

# Why Lap Dancing Is for You

*We don't care how big or small, short or tall, you are. Any girl can lap dance. We all have something to show off, whether it's beautiful breasts, lovely long legs, a big booty, or long, silky hair.*

Lap dancing is hot right now. All the celebs are doing it. Classes are springing up everywhere. . . . Everyone's caught the bug.

It's easy to see why. Not only will lap dancing put extra heat into your love life and help you get your dream body; it'll also send your confidence right through the roof.

After all, what could be more empowering than having your man just where you want him—begging for more, and bound by your rules?

When you give your lap dance, you'll be the one in control. Your man needs to know that you lay down the law. If you don't want him to touch you during your performance, let him know.

You make the rules, sister! He'll be so intoxicated by what he's seeing that he'll be putty in your hands.

# Getting in Shape the Fun Way

Lap dancing is the red-hot fitness craze that's sweeping the nation. A-list celebs like Carmen Electra have already recognized its body-sculpting potential. And now it's your turn, baby!

Do a little warm-up, grab a chair, and get ready to get flirty. The routines in this book have been professionally choreographed to help you get in shape while turning up the heat.

We recommend that you practice a routine a week and perform it for your man over the weekend. When you've mastered all five routines and thirty-five moves, you can use what you've learned to choreograph your own.

The moves that follow hit all the major areas: stomach, legs, arms, and butt. Practice them for half an hour or so every other day and you'll notice the toning effects within weeks.

Your appreciation of the way your body moves will also improve. How you choose to put this to use is entirely up to you. . . .

So if you think working out has to be a drag, it's time to think again. Let's get ready to lap dance!

# Fashion and Style Tips

First things first. What to wear? Check out the five things to remember when thinking about fashion for your lap dance. Then immerse yourself in our Peekaboo Girls' opinions on what's hot and what's not. . . .

1. Use your imagination. Anything that makes an impact is good. Think glamour, think naughtiness, think outrageously sexy. Perhaps you could customize your outfit to add some extra spice. Or why not think about uniforms and costumes?

2. Your outfit should allow you to move freely and should be easy to remove. When you lap dance, it should look effortless. You don't want to be restricted in your movements or spend time struggling to take things off. Practice removing your outfit before you perform to ensure there are no embarrassing hitches.

3. Give a lot of thought to your choice of footwear. A pair of high heels or thigh-high boots could provide the spark that sets your man on fire.

4. Don't forget to accessorize. Some gorgeous jewelry could really look amazing against your naked skin.

5. You might want to talk to your man about what he likes before you perform. This is a great way to get to know his most intimate desires and will make the experience one you both remember.

The cutest of the girls, Girly Girl Pink loves wearing her hair in curls and being nice to sweet animals like the hunky man in her life. She's flirty and coy, and so is her routine.

Baby dolls or feather-trimmed nightgowns, coupled with frilly edged French panties and a matching camisole, create a delicious look.

A feather boa plays a flirty part in her routine.

She wears a pink garter with ribbons in case her man decides she deserves a little financial reward for her performance.

Pink and feathery mules are her footwear of choice.

The poutiest of the girls, Babelicious Girl Blue knows she's the most gorgeous gal in the room. She performs her routine like a glamorous fashion model walking the runway.

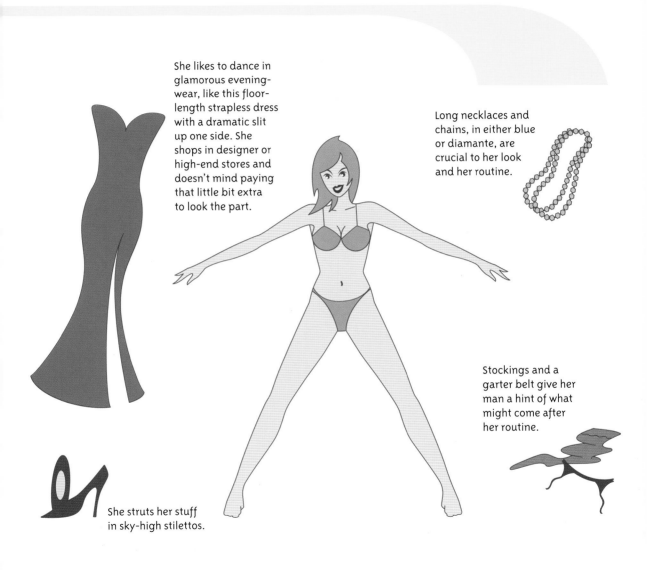

She likes to dance in glamorous evening-wear, like this floor-length strapless dress with a dramatic slit up one side. She shops in designer or high-end stores and doesn't mind paying that little bit extra to look the part.

Long necklaces and chains, in either blue or diamante, are crucial to her look and her routine.

Stockings and a garter belt give her man a hint of what might come after her routine.

She struts her stuff in sky-high stilettos.

The most musical of the girls, Go-Go Girl Green will sing and dance to almost anything. She performs her routine energetically and pays great attention to her choice of soundtrack.

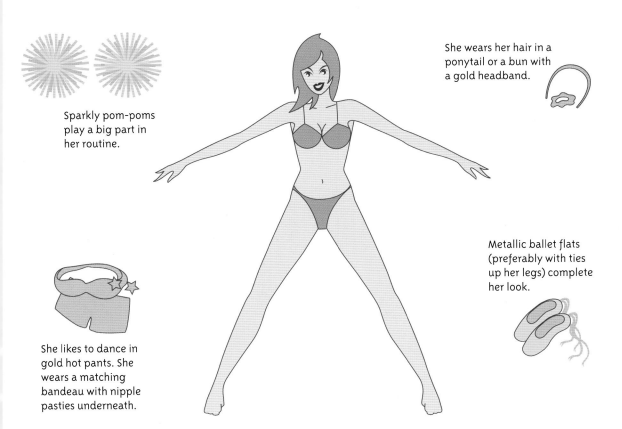

Sparkly pom-poms play a big part in her routine.

She wears her hair in a ponytail or a bun with a gold headband.

Metallic ballet flats (preferably with ties up her legs) complete her look.

She likes to dance in gold hot pants. She wears a matching bandeau with nipple pasties underneath.

The most fun loving of the girls, Party Girl Purple is the life and soul of the party. She performs her lap dance in the most attention-grabbing way imaginable.

She likes to dance in a short, low-cut party dress that leaves very little to the imagination. Bright colors that draw maximum attention are Party Girl Purple's weapons of choice.

A sexy leopard-print thong and push-up bra (it's very important that her man be able to see the straps before she takes off her dress!) complete her look.

A bottle of champagne plays a sparkling role in her routine.

High, strappy sandals or wedges provide the effect she's looking for.

The most badly behaved of all the girls, Bad Girl Black is oh so very naughty. She's a witchy woman with a raunchy routine.

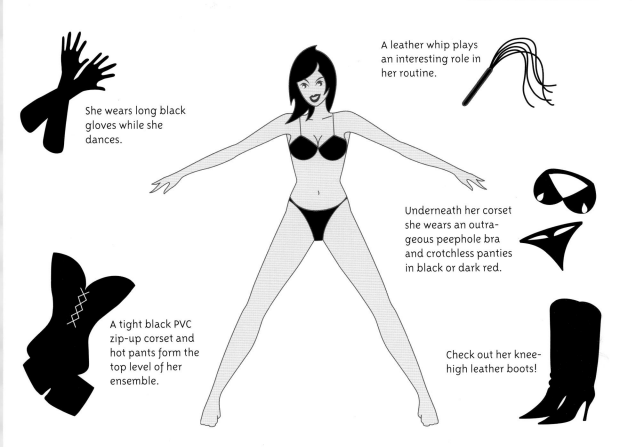

A leather whip plays an interesting role in her routine.

She wears long black gloves while she dances.

Underneath her corset she wears an outrageous peephole bra and crotchless panties in black or dark red.

A tight black PVC zip-up corset and hot pants form the top level of her ensemble.

Check out her knee-high leather boots!

# Setting the Scene for Your Lap Dance

Before you perform your routine, you'll want to make sure everything feels just right. Part of that is ensuring that you feel comfortable about where you dance. Before you strut your stuff, put your interior design hat on and set the stage for your man's seduction.

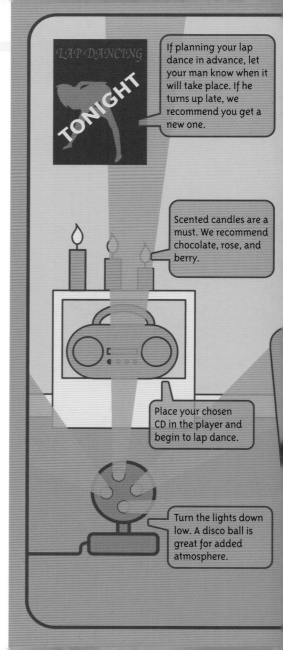

LAP DANCING

TONIGHT

If planning your lap dance in advance, let your man know when it will take place. If he turns up late, we recommend you get a new one.

Scented candles are a must. We recommend chocolate, rose, and berry.

Place your chosen CD in the player and begin to lap dance.

Turn the lights down low. A disco ball is great for added atmosphere.

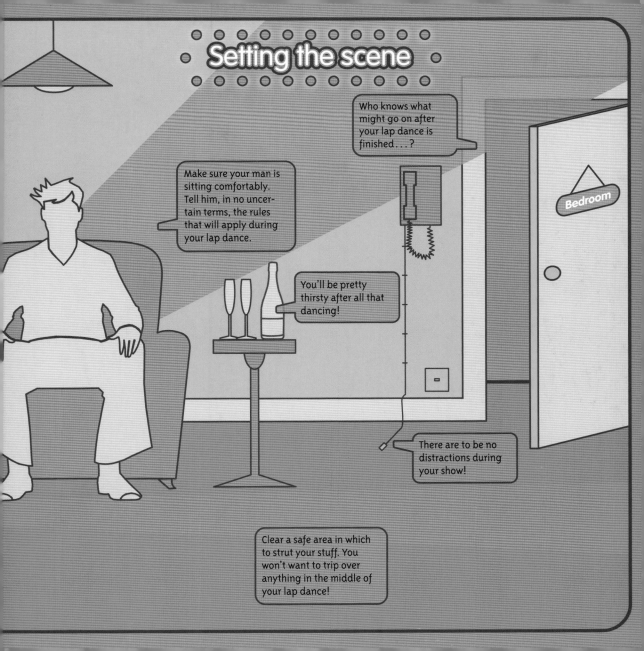

# Nine Foxy Lap-Dancing Secrets

Remember these truths. They'll never let you down. Follow them religiously and thou shalt not regret it.

1. Practice makes perfect. The more you hone your routine, the more natural it will feel when you perform for your man.

2. When performing for your man, maintain eye contact at all times. Little tricks like these are the ones that will make him go completely gaga.

3. Tease and tantalize your man by coming close and then drawing away at the very last moment.

4. Make sure your outfit is easy to remove before you perform. Imagine how frustrating it would be if you had to struggle to get something off at a key point in your routine.

5. Run your hands over your body and your man's eyes will follow.

6. Gently flick your hair over your man's face as you perform and he'll really start to get turned on.

7. Why not practice with your friends for extra fun and encouragement?

8. Perform moves that draw attention to your sexiest features. If you've got a big booty, then shake it. If you've got gorgeous breasts, then thrust them into your man's face. If you've got long legs, then stretch them out. Every girl's got something to flaunt. Confidence is sexy, so celebrate what you've got and show it off!

9. Slowly does it—savor the moment and draw out the moves for maximum effect.

# Before You Lap Dance

Can't wait to start dancing, huh? Easy, tiger. There are just a few more things we need to tell you. . . .

Every lap-dancing session should begin with a warm-up routine. It's important to prepare your body and stretch your muscles to minimize the chance of injury or strain.

We have grouped the following moves into routines by the five Peekaboo Girls. Each routine matches a particular girl's personality. If you identify very strongly with a certain girl, why not perform her routine? Otherwise you can pick and mix moves from all the girls to make your own routine.

A standard routine includes between five and ten moves. We think the ideal formula is to devote two moves to making your entrance, two to flaunting it, two to getting up close and personal, and one to your big exit.

The trick is to link each move with the next so that it flows perfectly. When you perform for your man, your routine should appear absolutely seamless.

To extend your routine, we suggest adding extra up-close-and-personal moves from other girls' routines.

Oh, and just one more thing. Once you're ready to perform your routine, you should think about music. Choose one of your favorite tracks first. As your confidence grows, you'll get a feel for combining songs with moves and developing a more choreographed routine.

Okay, that's it. Now let's have some real fun. . . .

## Remember to Keep Safety in Mind!

Please make sure to warm up before you attempt the routines in this book. If, for any reason, you are physically incapable of moderate exercise, you should not attempt the dance moves. Consult a doctor or specialist if you are unsure.

Chairs that tip back, fold, or are on wheels should not be used to perform any of the routines in this book.

# Strike a Pose

**Every girl knows the importance of making a big entrance. Don't walk up to your man at the start of your performance in a humdrum way. Look at him seductively as you strut, prance, and shimmy over. Leave him wanting more—much more!**

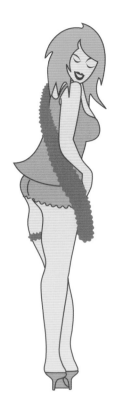

1. Start with your back to your man. Don't move for a few seconds. Strike a pose and let him drink you in. Cross one leg over the other while looking back at him with a coy, girly expression.

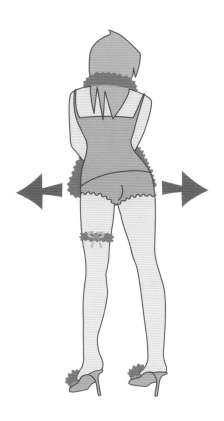

2. Wrap the feather boa around your neck slowly and seductively. Begin to gently sway your hips side to side in time with the music.

3. Finish by looking back over your shoulder and giving your man a naughty wink. That's it, baby! Now you're really feeling it.

# Walk the Walk

By now you should have your man's undivided attention. Let's keep it that way. This move will make the short journey from floor to armchair pass like a dream.

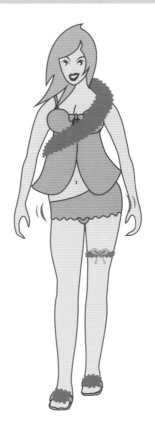

1. Turn and start to walk toward your man. Bask in the glow as his eyes move over your body. Put a sway into every step you take. Work those hips, gorgeous!

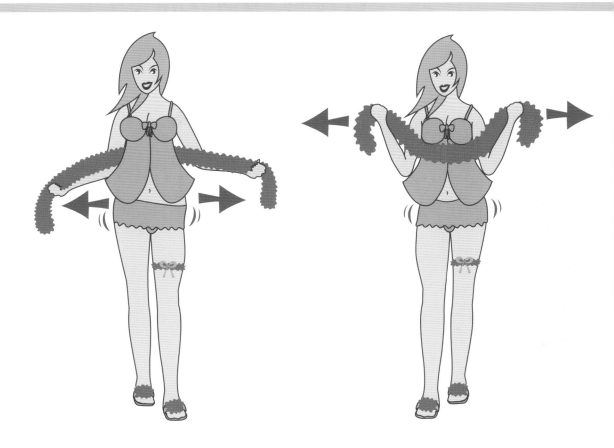

2. Begin to pull your feather boa sexily right and left behind your back as if drying yourself off after a sexy midnight swim.

3. Now move the feather boa to the front and repeat step 2, bringing your arms closer together to show off your breasts.

# Bootylicious

Okay. So you've reached your man's chair. But what now? Don't panic, honey! This move is sure to get him hot under the collar.

1. Turn around to face away from your man, and hold one end of the feather boa in your right hand.

2. Drop your boa and give it
   a little "Oops!"

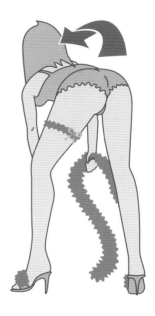

3. As you bend gracefully to
   pick it up again, hoist your
   sexy butt in the air and
   show off your frilly panties.
   Mmm-mmm! My, oh, my,
   you're lookin' good!

29

# Tickling His Fancy

This move is designed to give your audience a treat. And don't worry if you're a little ticklish. You can giggle if you want to. It's your show and you make the rules.

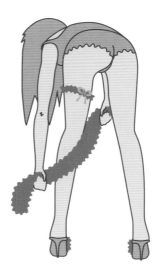

1. Bend over and pick up the other end of the feather boa.

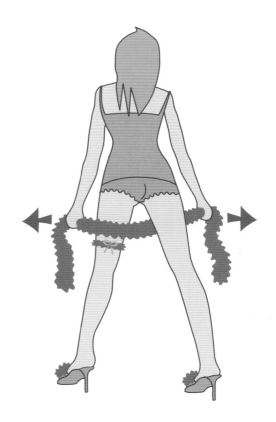

2. Run the boa suggestively back and forth between your legs. Even if he's not the sharpest tool in the box, he'll get the idea.

3. Seductively raise yourself back to your feet while moving the boa from side to side between your legs.

# Sitting Comfortably?

Don't take a seat next to your man,
by him, or near him. Take a seat on him,
as if he's part of the armchair. Then
recline, relax, and get comfortable.

1. Slowly lower yourself onto
your man's lap.

2. Tilt your head back to expose your neck, and begin slowly wiggling and gently jiggling against him. Perform little circular movements with your hips. Let's make this the best seat in the house.

3. Wrap your arm around his neck (give him a good view of your breasts) and whisper something seductive in his ear.

33

# The Kinky Kick Start

Now that you're feeling nice and comfortable, let's really bring out your inner lap dancer. This move will show once and for all that you can kick it with the best of them.

1. Tilt your head back again, moving those hips all the time.

2. Start to kick your legs in the air one at a time.

3. Use this kicking motion to get back to your feet without a pause in your routine. Can-can you do it?

# Bye-bye, Handsome

**Wow! What a journey. And it's not over yet. Perform this move and you'll leave your man with something to remember you by.**

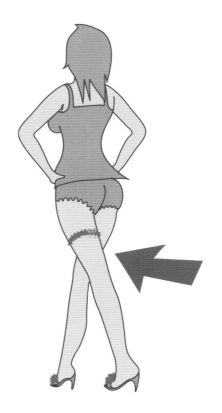

1. Place your hands on your hips, arch your back, thrust your breasts out, and walk slowly away.

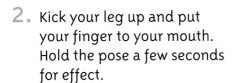

2. Kick your leg up and put your finger to your mouth. Hold the pose a few seconds for effect.

3. Walk off with a wiggle of the hips, looking coyly over your shoulder as you go.

# The Poser

**Red carpets. Photo shoots. Your picture all over every magazine from New York to San Francisco. Star quality, baby, that's what you've got.**

**It's time to strike a pose!**

1. Facing your man, push your hips out and move them round and round in a perfect circle—the bigger the better. This move is not only super sexy; it's also great for your abs.

**2.** Place your right hand on your right hip as you continue to swivel.

**3.** Point your left foot out and come to a halt. Look up. You're like something out of *Vogue*, baby. Graciously accept the adulation of your audience.

# When Will I Be Famous?

When is a walk more than just a walk? When it includes equal measures strut, thrust, pout, and wiggle, we say.

So when you walk toward your man, don't just walk toward your man. Do it with attitude, and watch his eyes widen as he anticipates your next move.

1. Place your hands on your hips, arch your back, and thrust your breasts out.

2. Strut toward your man as if you're an "It girl" basking in the glare of the world's paparazzi. As you do so, pass your jewelry through your fingers.

3. You've arrived at your destination. Give it a little wiggle to celebrate.

# Look into My Eyes...

**This one's from the belly-dancing school of seduction.**

**You'll feel the toning effects in your legs, butt, and abs; your man will feel them in his...ahem. We'd better stop there.**

1. With your feet slightly apart, bend your knees.

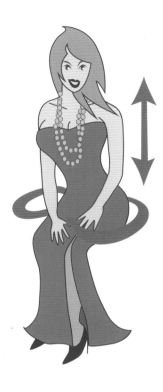

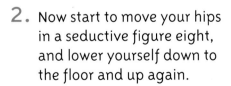

2. Now start to move your hips in a seductive figure eight, and lower yourself down to the floor and up again.

3. Run your fingers through your hair as you move your other hand up and down your body. By this stage your man will be in the early stages of hypnosis. What you do with him now is up to you.

# The Puppet Master

This playful move guides your man's eyes wherever you want them to go. Think of him as your little puppet on a string.

1. Begin by moving your hips side to side sexily and lowering yourself to the floor.

2. Stretch your left leg out and run your hands along it seductively.

3. Whip your head back and forth, sending your hair over your face. Delicious!

# Breast in Show

Now's the time to get really naughty. With this move the secret is to keep it slow and sexy. Give your man a peep and he'll enjoy a real eyeful.

**1.** Walk seductively those last couple of steps toward your man.

2. Move between his knees, lean forward, and place your hands on either side of him.

3. Bring your breasts close to his face, and move them from side to side and up and down. If you keep it cool, you'll really heat up the room.

# Legs o' Heaven

This move is designed to show off your lovely long legs while reminding your man who's boss.

Please bear in mind that step 1 requires a high level of flexibility. Oh, and whatever you do, don't forget to wax the night before.

1. Stand gracefully facing your man. Put all your weight on your standing foot and lift the other over his shoulder and onto the back of the chair.

2. Begin to gently sway your hips from side to side.

3. Now rub your hands over your body and play with your hair. In this elevated position, you're so out of his league, sister! Make sure to let him know it.

# Pout It Out

Here's a finishing move that'll display your star quality to devastating effect. Unless we're very much mistaken, it'll leave your man positively weak with desire.

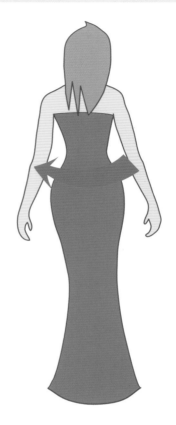

**1.** Spin around until you are facing away from your man.

2. Do a little catwalk, working those hips for all you're worth.

3. Turn around and bend forward, pushing your breasts together with your arms. Now blow your man a little kiss and stride away, diva style.

# Check Me Out

All revved up and ready to go? Well, okay, then. This is a great move to start with. It'll have you jumping around like a super-sexy cheerleader.

**1.** Start with your back to your man.

2. Bend over so your pom-poms touch the floor, and give your fanny a flirty wiggle. Now slowly straighten up while rolling your pom-poms one over the other.

3. When you're close to standing straight, do the most spectacular jumping jack you can do. He won't know what hit him.

# Little Miss Mischief

This is a real flirty way to make the trip to your man's chair. It'll test your coordination, but get it right and the razzmatazz factor will hit the roof.

1. Keep your pom-poms up by your breasts.

2. Start to walk backward, wiggling your bottom and shaking your pom-poms as you do so.

3. Keep going, and look over first one shoulder and then the other, pouting all the time. Rotate your hips and roll your pom-poms first on one side and then the other, as you go.

# The Tail Feather

This move will show off your luscious rear to the max. If you broke it down into its component parts, you'd be left with three parts naughtiness, two parts jiggling, and four parts flauntiness.

**1.** Keep your back to your man, and lower yourself down onto your haunches, shaking your pom-poms above your head.

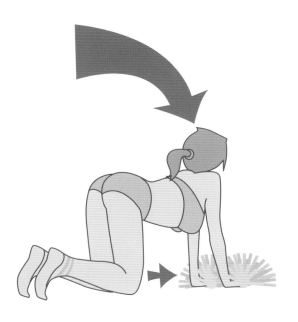

2. Now place your hands on the floor and walk them out until you're stretched out on all fours.

3. To finish, arch your back and jiggle your butt around. Looks peachy from where we're standing!

# Peep Show

This is a move for the ultraflexible.
It'll stretch your hamstrings and tone
your butt to the max.

Plus it'll give your man a view he's
not likely to forget in a hurry.

1. Come up to standing.
   Arch your back a little so
   your butt pops out.

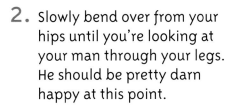

2. Slowly bend over from your hips until you're looking at your man through your legs. He should be pretty darn happy at this point.

3. Now slowly straighten back up. As you do so, remove your top. That'll give him something to think about.

# Bump and Grind

We bet you're pretty out of breath by now. So let's get comfortable and have a little rest. Hmm...Seems like all the chairs are taken. Where to park it? We have an idea.

**1.** Still facing away from your man, edge toward him and place your hands on the edge of his chair or his knees.

2. Now gently push yourself down into his lap.

3. Grind and wiggle your butt tantalizingly. Make sure to keep leaning slightly forward. He still hasn't seen your breasts, and we want to keep it that way for a little longer.

# Ride 'Em, Cowgirl

If you're dancing to a slow song, treat this move like a pretty, prancing performance. For fast songs (the ones Go-Go Girl Green likes best of all), it should be a red-hot, raunchy rodeo.

**1.** Stay in the saddle, honey, and start bouncing along to the beat of the music.

**2.** Keep on bouncing, and wave your pom-poms in the air (shouting "Yeehaw!" is entirely optional at this stage, but we've tried it and found it loads of fun).

**3.** Lean back until your man can nearly see your breasts, but then, as he starts to get really excited, spring onto your feet. Just a little longer, handsome.

# The Big Reveal

Every good boy deserves a treat. This move serves up exactly what your man has been dreaming about for the last few minutes.

**1.** Spin around until you're facing your man but covering your breasts with your pom-poms.

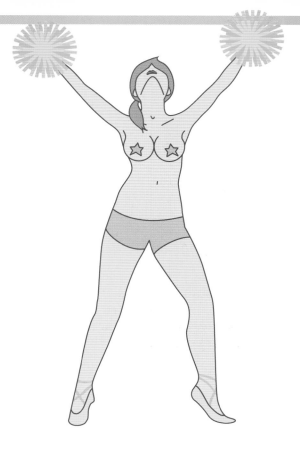

2. Start to roll your pom-poms tantalizingly.

3. The moment has arrived! Keep rolling your pom-poms, but bring them higher and higher until your nipple pasties and the obvious are revealed. Now throw your head back and strike a pose.

65

# Wave Hello

When performing this move, imagine a wave passing through your body from your tippie-toes up. Your man will love what he sees, and your tummy will get a toning as well.

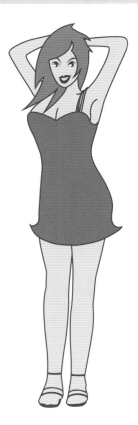

**1.** Start by facing your man with your feet together and your hands in your hair.

**2.** Sway your hips back and forth in time with the music, and lower yourself to the ground (you should feel this one in your tummy muscles and thighs).

**3.** Hook your finger under your bra strap and pull it off your shoulder if you're feeling really flirty.

# Catwalk Crazy

**This is a provocative move that requires you to step forward and get closer to your audience.**

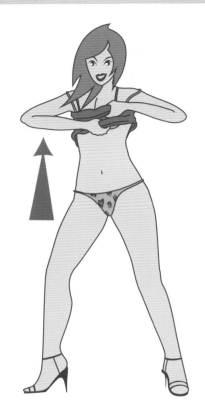

**1.** As you come back up to standing, remove your dress to reveal your underwear.

**2.** Hit the catwalk and strut toward your man.

**3.** You've arrived at your destination. Give it a little wiggle to celebrate.

# A Perfect Circle

Using a piece of charcoal, Michelangelo drew the perfect circle to prove his gifts as an artist. You'll be doing the same to prove yours as a lap dancer, using your heavenly hips and randy rear.

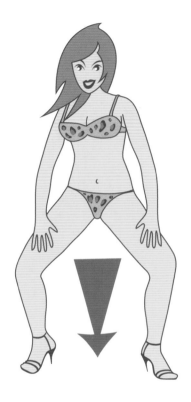

1. Facing your man, place your feet slightly apart and bend your knees. This move is great exercise for your glutes and quads (your butt and thighs, in other words).

2. Now push your hips out and move them round and round in the perfect circle—the bigger the better.

3. Caress your hair and breasts with your hands. If he's still able to speak, your man might like to compliment you on your artistic ability.

# Carpet Curves

Show a little curve and make him fall in love with this lazy little number. It's the female form at its best... flat-out sexy!

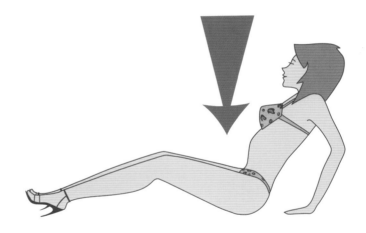

**1.** Lower yourself to the floor.

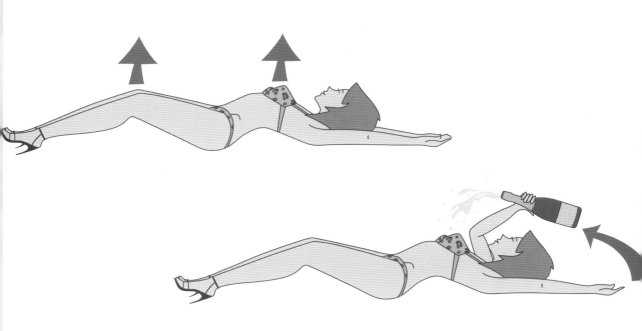

2. Keeping your feet together, slowly lift your knees and arch your back. Can you feel it in your abs?

3. Reach backward and pick up your carefully positioned champagne bottle. Proceed to pour some of the lovely bubbly stuff over your chest. Place the bottle back on the floor.

# Let's Get This Party Started

Now, we wouldn't want that champagne to go to waste, would we?

This move takes a little practice. Get the hang of it and you'll put a sparkle in your man's eye.

1. Place your legs between your man's, and support yourself with your hands on the back of his chair.

2. Press your body against him and give him permission to lick off that delicious champagne.

3. Now slide all the way down him until you are kneeling on the floor. Is it us, or is it getting hot in here?

# Mischievous Massage

**CAUTION!** Things are about to get seriously naughty. We suggest you perform the first part of this move very gently. We wouldn't want your man to get totally carried away, now, would we?

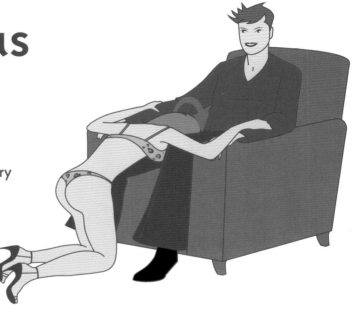

**1.** Lean forward and massage your man's groin with the top of your head.

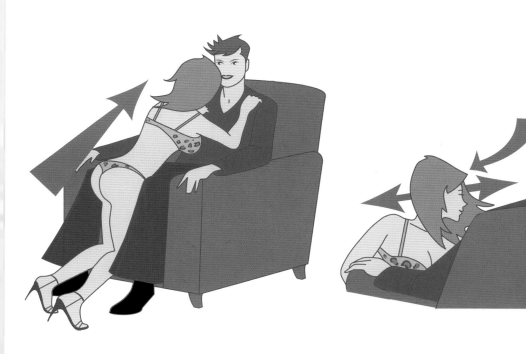

2. Climb back up him, gripping onto his shirt like a cat (keep your eyes open for Party Girl Purple's final move, which takes the feline theme even further).

3. Slide back down him again into the kneeling position, and swing your head from one side to the other, sending your hair over your face with wanton abandon.

# Tiger, Tiger

**This is a very sexy move that shows you're not scared to be an animal in the bedroom.**

**Welcome to the jungle. It's time to take your man on a wild adventure.**

**1.** Kneeling between your man's legs, run your hands up and down his thighs.

2. Look up at him and make
eye contact. Begin to crawl
backward like the untamed
animal you are, keeping your
eyes on him all the time.

3. To finish, rise up onto your
knees with a shimmying
motion and throw your head
back, revealing your neck.

# Whip It Up

**With this move you'll be in control. Your man will be amazed. He always thought you were such a sweet and innocent girl. Guess we've all got a darker side!**

1. Start by standing with your side facing your man. And yes, that is a whip; your eyes aren't playing tricks on you.

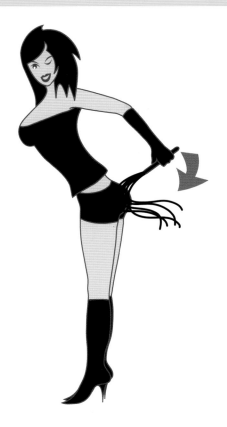

2. Bend forward slightly and give your man a naughty little look. Now give your butt a tap with the whip—who's been a bad girl?

3. Repeat on your other buttock and give your man a look like you're really digging it. You can use the whip as gently or as hard as you feel necessary. Just how naughty have you been?

81

# Sexual Predator

What's the point of waiting for your prey to come to you? If you want something bad enough, you'll hunt it down. The tasty morsel of the day just happens to be your hunky man.

1. First get down on all fours facing your man. Keep your eyes fixed on his the whole time.

2. Start to crawl toward him. Imagine you're a panther. Move slinkily and sinuously. You might even want to try a little roar.

3. You've reached your prey. Rub yourself up against his legs to show how happy you are. That's just purrrrfect. . . .

# Kinky Boots

This move is similar to Mischievous Massage (pages 76–77), only it's performed while standing up—giving you the perfect opportunity to remove your knee-high leather boots.

By the way, if there's a man alive who isn't a fan of knee-high leather boots, we've yet to meet him.

**1.** First stand up and face your man.

2. Bending at the hips while keeping your legs straight, lean forward and push his legs apart.

3. While massaging his groin with your head, unzip your sexy boots and kick them away. Pretty steamy? Well, brace yourself, because it's all about to get way, way hotter.

# Red Hot Pants

This move lets you get a little more comfortable. All the thought you gave to your choice of underwear will now pay off big time.

1. Stand up between your man's legs, facing away from him.

2. Pushing your bottom toward him while moving your hips in a circular motion, pull off your hot pants and give them a flirty kick across the room.

3. Tap your butt suggestively with the whip and hand it over to your man. Make it clear that he can use it only when you tell him to. We don't want him getting ideas above his station, do we?

# Naughty, Naughty

We reckon your man will be foaming at the mouth by the time you get to this move. But this is your party and you're not done with him yet. Patience is a virtue he's just gonna have to learn.

**1.** Standing in front of your man, place your right foot between his legs.

2. Very slowly remove your zip-up corset and look on as his tongue hits the floor.

3. Turn your right hip slightly toward him and (using only suggestive eye movements) let him know that you would like a little spanking with the whip.

# Venus Leg Trap

**When you perform this move, your man will be one willing fly. It's absolutely deadly and will render him completely defenseless. Plus it's pretty darn athletic. Yummy, yummy!**

1. Place one foot and then the other on your man's chair to the sides of his hips.

2. Now sit down in his lap and wrap your legs around his neck.

3. Clasping him between your legs, transfer your weight onto your arms and grind and rub up against his body.

# Follow My Leader

This move is guaranteed to drive him wild. Look at his handsome face! See how happy he is? It's like something out of his dreams, so he'd better make the most of it.

1. Slide yourself off your man's lap and down onto your knees (gently does it).

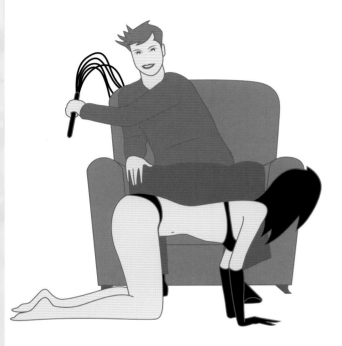

2. Turn around, hitch your butt up high, and offer yourself up for another little spanking with the whip.

3. Begin to crawl away from him, working your hips and butt all the way. Peek over your shoulder and give him your most suggestive look. Try crawling like this all the way to the bedroom. . . .

# Good-bye, Gorgeous

**Well, it's been fun, hon, but we've gotta split. Before we go, though, there are a few more things we'd like to say. So wipe the tears from those gorgeous peepers and listen up. . . .**

Now, remember what we said way back at the start: this is your lap dance and you're the one in control.

So if you make a little mistake while performing your routine, don't worry your pretty head about it. Just continue shaking it like the lap-dancing goddess you are. Chances are he won't have noticed anything anyway.

Same goes if you forget your next move mid routine. It's not the end of the world. Keep on shimmying and maybe strike a few poses until it comes back to you. He'll be none the wiser.

The most important thing is that you have loads of fun. 'Cause from where we're standing, you've got it, baby, so you'd better flaunt it.

*Peekaboo*

GOOD LUCK, SWEETIE!!
GIRLY GIRL PINK
xxx

Don't be a stranger, girl!!
Party-Girl Purple ☺

You're a real superstar!!!
Babelicious Girl Blue
xx

We love you!!
Go-Go Girl Green
x x x x

DRIVE HIM WILD, SUGAR!
BAD GIRL BLACK
x

# Index